COMPARING ANIMAL TRAITS

CALIFORNIA CONDORS

WIDE-WINGED SOARING BIRDS

LAURA HAMILTON WAXMAN

Lerner Publications ◆ Minneapolis

For Brett, my wonderful Californian friend

Lerner Publications Company
A division of Lerner Publishing Group, Inc.
241 First Avenue North
Minneapolis, MN 55401 USA

For reading levels and more information, look up this title at www.lernerbooks.com.

Photo Acknowledgments

The images in this book are used with the permission of:
© age fotostock/SuperStock, p. 1; © John Cancalosi/Alamy, p. 4; © Andriy Blokhin/Dreamstime.com, p. 5; US Fish and Wildlife Service, p. 6; © Feverpitched/Dreamstime.com, p. 7 (top); © Michael Elliott/Dreamstime.com, p. 7 (bottom); © Tokumi/Gin tonic/Wikimedia Commons, p. 8; © 4028mdk09/Wikimedia Commons (CC BY-SA 3.0), p. 9 (right); Michael Durham/Minden Pictures/Newscom, p. 9 (left); © Glenn Bartley/All Canada Photos/SuperStock, p. 10; © Erni/Shutterstock.com, p. 11; © Laura Westlund/Independent Picture Service, p. 12; © CO Leong/Shutterstock.com, p. 13; © Glen Tepke, p. 14; © Tom Ulrich/Visuals Unlimited, Inc., p. 15 (top); © Terry Gray/Wikimedia Commons (CC BY-SA 2.0), p. 15 (bottom); © Wing-Chi Poon/Wikimedia Commons (CC BY-SA 2.5), p. 16; © John Cancalosi/ardea.com/Pan/Pantheon/SuperStock, p. 17 (bottom left); © iStockphoto.com/epantha, p. 17 (bottom right); © Universal Images Group/SuperStock, p. 18; © iStockphoto.com/RealWorldStu, p. 19 (top); © Anthony Mercieca/SuperStock, p. 19 (bottom); © McDonald Wildlife Photography/Animals Animals, p. 20; © Minden Pictures/SuperStock, p. 21 (top); © Paul S. Wolf/Shutterstock.com, p. 21 (bottom); © Steve Byland/Shutterstock.com, p. 22; © iStockphoto.com/Len Jellicoe, p. 23 (bottom left); © cliff collings/Shutterstock.com, p. 23 (bottom right); © imageBROKER/Alamy, p. 24; Joseph Brandt/US Fish and Wildlife Service (CC BY 2.0), pp. 25 (top), 27 (bottom left); © iStockphoto.com/kojihirano, p. 25 (bottom); © kansasphoto/flickr.com (CC BY 2.0), p. 26; Martin Harvey/NHPA/Photoshot/Newscom, p. 27 (bottom right); © iStockphoto.com/SteveByland, p. 28; © Ardea/Sid Roberts/Animals Animals, p. 29 (top); © Steve and Dave Maslowski/Science Source, p. 29 (bottom).

Front cover: © John Cancalosi/ardea.com/Pan/Pantheon/SuperStock.
Back cover: © Minden Pictures/SuperStock.

Main body text set in Calvert MT Std 12/18. Typeface provided by Monotype Typography.

Library of Congress Cataloging-in-Publication Data

Cataloging-in-Publication Data for *California Condors: Wide-Winged Soaring Birds* is on file at the Library of Congress.
ISBN: 978-1-4677-9512-8 (LB)
ISBN: 978-1-4677-9639-2 (PB)
ISBN: 978-1-4677-9640-8 (EB)

Manufactured in the United States of America
1 – BP – 12/31/15

TABLE OF CONTENTS

MEET THE CALIFORNIA CONDOR

A California condor soars high in the sky on its wide wings. Its sharp eyes look for dead animals to eat. California condors are a kind of bird. Other kinds of animals you may know include insects, reptiles, fish, amphibians, and mammals.

All birds share certain features. Birds are vertebrates—animals with backbones. Birds have feathers and a beak. Birds are warm-blooded, which means they make their own body heat. Their body temperature stays the same, even when the temperature around them changes. Birds also lay hard-shelled eggs. California condors share these traits with other birds.

A California condor has powerful eyesight.

California condors are one of two condor species in the world. The other is the Andean condor of South America. Both condors are endangered. Just thirty years ago, fewer than 25 California condors lived in the wild. Since then, people have been working hard to save them. These days, there are about 230 California condors in the wild.

CHAPTER 1

WHAT DO CALIFORNIA CONDORS LOOK LIKE?

California condors are the largest wild birds in North America. They weigh between 18 and 30 pounds (8.2 and 14 kilograms). They have a huge wingspan of up to 10 feet (3 meters). Long feathers stick out from the end of each wing. The feathers look like fingers. This wing shape allows condors to glide easily on warm, rising currents of air.

Do you see the fingerlike feathers at the ends of this California condor's wings?

California condors have traits that help them feed on dead animals.

California condor feathers are mostly black. Under their wings are large patches of white feathers. Their reddish-orange head and neck do not have feathers. When the birds eat, these body parts often get covered in blood. They are easier to clean because they are featherless. Condors have a sharp, hooked beak for tearing apart meat. Near the bottom of their throat is a pouch called a crop. It can store food for days at a time.

DID YOU KNOW?
The skin on the head and neck of a California condor turns PINK when the bird gets excited.

CALIFORNIA CONDORS VS. STELLER'S SEA EAGLES

A soaring Steller's sea eagle circles above a river full of swimming salmon. Steller's sea eagles are large, brown and white birds of Russia and Japan. They weigh 13 to 20 pounds (5.9 to 9.1 kg). Their wingspan can be up to 8 feet (2.4 m) wide.

Steller's sea eagles have the same wing shape as California condors. And both birds have a short, wedge-shaped tail. The birds use their tails in flight to change direction or slow down.

Steller's sea eagles have a pointed, hooked beak for ripping into meat. They have sharp **talons** for grasping salmon. California condors also have talons. But they are not as sharp.

A Steller's sea eagle soars.

COMPARE IT!

CALIFORNIA CONDORS

VS.

STELLER'S SEA EAGLES

CALIFORNIA CONDORS		STELLER'S SEA EAGLES
LONG, WITH FINGERLIKE FEATHERS	◄ WING SHAPE ►	LONG, WITH FINGERLIKE FEATHERS
10 FEET (3 M)	◄ MAXIMUM WINGSPAN ►	**8 FEET** (2.4 M)
Yes	◄ TALONS? ►	Yes

CALIFORNIA CONDORS VS. GREEN-HEADED TANAGERS

A green-headed tanager hops from branch to branch searching for insects. Green-headed tanagers are much smaller than California condors. They weigh just 0.6 ounces (18 grams). And they're only 5 inches (13 centimeters) long from beak to tail.

Unlike condors, green-headed tanagers are colorful birds. Patches of green, yellow, blue, orange, and black feathers cover their round bodies. Their short wings are suited for fast flapping instead of soaring. Their tail is shaped like a fan.

A green-headed tanager perches on a branch.

A green-headed tanager's beak is not hooked like a condor's. It's small and pointed for eating fruit and insects. The toes and claws of these birds are thin and delicate for gripping branches. In comparison, the feet of California condors are thick and sturdy.

CHAPTER 2

WHERE DO CALIFORNIA CONDORS LIVE?

California condors seek two types of habitat. They mostly live in mountains with rocky cliffs, canyons, and forests. But they search for food in open areas with low grass. These two habitats are often far apart.

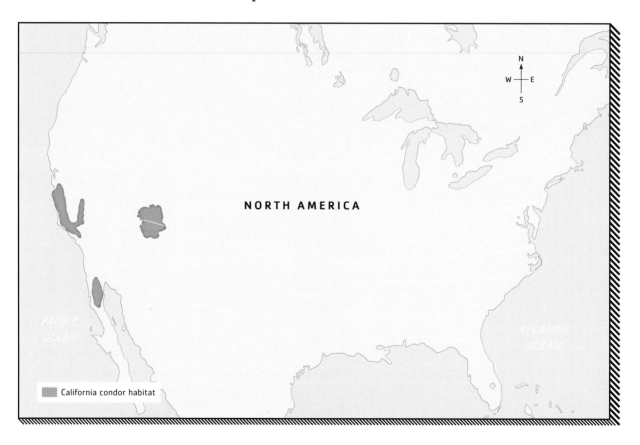

N
W E
S

NORTH AMERICA

PACIFIC OCEAN

ATLANTIC OCEAN

■ California condor habitat

The California condors' rocky habitat provides them with shelter. Shaded cliffs and mountain forests protect the birds from the hot sun and bad weather. California condors depend on their open habitat to spot food on the ground from above. Short grass makes it easier to find the dead animals they feed on. Condors also need plenty of space to lift off in flight. These heavy birds must take a running start to get off the ground.

CALIFORNIA CONDORS VS. BLACK SWIFTS

A hungry black swift flies toward a swarm of flying ants. It captures the insects in its small, pointed beak and swallows them. Like California condors, black swifts live high in the mountains. They find shelter on steep cliffs behind waterfalls and in small, damp caves. Here they are hidden from predators, such as falcons.

Do you see the black swifts flying near this waterfall?

A black swift in its nest

Like condors, black swifts need open space to find food. But they don't find it on the ground. Black swifts catch their food in the air, often over open bodies of water. Black swifts eat flies, termites, and other flying insects. Like condors, they sometimes fly long distances from where they shelter to where they hunt.

DID YOU KNOW?

Black swifts spend most of their time in the air. They **REST** only at their nest site.

CALIFORNIA CONDORS VS. PURPLE GALLINULES

A purple gallinule flicks its tail feathers as it steps from one lily pad to another. Purple gallinules don't live high in the mountains like California condors do. Purple gallinules make their home in wetlands with slow-moving water. That includes swamps, marshes, and ponds.

Purple gallinules seek wetlands with plenty of floating plants. That's because the birds often walk on the plants in search of food in the water. Purple gallinules feed on the frogs, worms, snails, and fish in their habitat. They also eat plants that grow in and near water.

A purple gallinule searches for food.

COMPARE IT!

CALIFORNIA CONDORS

VS.

PURPLE GALLINULES

CALIFORNIA CONDORS		PURPLE GALLINULES
CLIFFS, CANYONS, MOUNTAIN FORESTS, AND OPEN GRASSLANDS	HABITAT	WETLANDS WITH FLOATING PLANTS
SOUTHWESTERN UNITED STATES AND BAJA, MEXICO	GEOGRAPHIC RANGE	SOUTHEASTERN UNITED STATES, MEXICO, AND SOUTH AMERICA

Yes	TRAVELS LONG DISTANCES TO FIND FOOD?	No

CHAPTER 3

CALIFORNIA CONDORS IN ACTION

A California condor soars over an open field in search of carrion. With its powerful eyesight, it spots a dead goat below. Then the condor quickly lands, walks up to the goat, and digs in with its sharp beak.

California condors are scavengers. Often the large, dead animals they eat have been killed by other animals. Condors may travel more than 100 miles (161 kilometers) in a single day to find food to eat. They often gather in groups around carrion. Together, they eat as much of the meat as they can.

These California condors have found a dead goat to eat.

DID YOU KNOW?
Condors are part of a fierce group of birds called **RAPTORS**, or birds of prey. Other raptors include eagles, owls, falcons, and vultures.

California condors can store up to 3 pounds (1.4 kg) of meat in their crop. They will digest this food later. If needed, they can survive for up to two weeks without finding more food.

Some of the carrion meat and blood gets on the condor's skin and in its feathers. But California condors are clean birds. They bathe often in pools of water. They also rub their head and neck against rocks, branches, and grass.

A California condor cleans itself in a pool of water.

CALIFORNIA CONDORS VS. TURKEY VULTURES

A turkey vulture flies low to the ground, sniffing for dead animals. Turkey vultures are scavengers like condors. Both birds gather in groups around the carrion. Turkey vultures don't just eat in groups though. They also live together in groups, as do California condors.

Both turkey vultures and California condors often sun themselves. They stretch their dark wings and soak in the sun's heat to warm up. The sun also dries their feathers if they get wet from rain or morning dew.

Turkey vultures eat a fish.

A turkey vulture suns itself on top of a cactus.

Like condors, turkey vultures have few predators. But turkey vultures have an interesting way of defending themselves. They will throw up if a predator such as an owl comes near. The terrible smell can scare the other animal away.

DID YOU KNOW?

Turkey vultures are one of the only bird species to rely heavily on their sense of **SMELL**. The part of their brain that controls smell is larger than in most other birds.

CALIFORNIA CONDORS VS. NORTHERN MOCKINGBIRDS

A northern mockingbird sits on top of a bush singing a new song. Northern mockingbirds are famous singers. They are known for imitating the songs of other birds. They even imitate sirens, barking dogs, and other sounds. They sing to mark their territory, warn of danger, and attract mates. In comparison, California condors can only hiss, grunt, and snort.

Northern mockingbirds are not soaring birds. They find their food by hopping along the ground or perching in a bush. Northern mockingbirds are omnivores. They eat everything from insects to plants.

Northern mockingbirds live alone or in pairs. They chase away other mockingbirds that enter their territory. They will even try to scare off dogs, cats, and people.

A northern mockingbird sings from a tree branch.

COMPARE IT!

CALIFORNIA CONDORS

VS.

NORTHERN MOCKINGBIRDS

DEAD ANIMALS ◄ MAIN FOOD ► **INSECTS AND PLANTS**

GRUNTS AND HISSES ◄ COMMUNICATION ► **IMITATES SOUNDS AND SONGS**

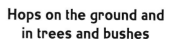

Soars high over the ground ◄ HOW IT FINDS FOOD ► Hops on the ground and in trees and bushes

CHAPTER 4

THE LIFE CYCLE OF CALIFORNIA CONDORS

California condors stay with the same mate for their entire lives. When it's time to lay eggs, the male and female pair looks for a good spot to nest. California condors don't build nests. They mostly lay eggs in natural holes in cliffs and rocky caves. Female condors lay one egg, which both parents incubate. After about eight weeks, the egg hatches. Out comes a chick covered in fluffy feathers. It weighs around 6 ounces (175 g).

A pair of California condors

A female California condor and her chick

Both parents feed their chick by regurgitating food. In about six months, the chick is big and strong enough to begin to fly. But it takes the young condor more than a year to learn to fly well and to find food by itself. Young California condors take a long time to grow up. They are ready to mate after six to eight years. In the wild, they live up to sixty years.

DID YOU KNOW?

Female California condors usually lay a **SINGLE EGG** every one or two years. That's one of the reasons the birds are still endangered.

CALIFORNIA CONDORS VS. WHITE-TAILED TROPICBIRDS

A white-tailed tropicbird dives from the sky into the ocean. It snatches a fish in its beak and gulps it down. White-tailed tropicbirds and California condors have a similar life cycle. Like condors, female tropicbirds lay one egg each breeding cycle. Their nests are shaded holes in cliffs and steep rock faces. Both the male and female take turns incubating the egg, which hatches after six weeks.

Both parents feed the chick by regurgitating fish. The chick is ready to fly after ten to twelve weeks. It will be fully grown and ready to mate by the time it's four years old. White-tailed tropicbirds live for about sixteen years.

White-tailed tropicbirds are swift fliers.

COMPARE IT!

CALIFORNIA CONDORS

VS.

WHITE-TAILED TROPICBIRDS

1 — NUMBER OF EGGS LAID ▶ — **1**

Holes and caves in cliffs ◀ LOCATION OF NEST ▶ Shaded holes in cliffs and rock faces

60 YEARS ◀ AVERAGE LIFE SPAN IN THE WILD ▶ **16 YEARS**

CALIFORNIA CONDORS VS. BROWN-HEADED COWBIRDS

A brown-headed cowbird walks across a log eating seeds and insects. Brown-headed cowbirds have a different life cycle than California condors. Male and female cowbirds don't form lasting pairs, and they don't raise their young. Instead, the female lays one to seven eggs in the nests of other birds. Then her job is done. She will go on to mate with other male cowbirds. Over the next two months, she'll lay around forty eggs.

Some birds shove cowbird eggs out of their nest. But most birds don't recognize the cowbird eggs. The birds incubate them along with their own eggs. The cowbird eggs hatch in less than two weeks, before most other eggs.

Do you see the spotted brown-headed cowbird eggs in this red-winged blackbird nest?

That means cowbird chicks get more food and attention than the chicks that hatch later. After one to two months, the young cowbirds leave to join a **flock** of other brown-headed cowbirds. They are fully grown after a year. Brown-headed cowbirds live for about sixteen years.

A blue-winged warbler (*right*) feeds a brown-headed cowbird chick (*left*).

CALIFORNIA CONDOR TRAIT CHART

This book introduces California condors and compares them to other birds. What other birds would you like to compare?

	WARM-BLOODED	FEATHERS	LAYS HARD-SHELLED EGGS	WIDE WINGSPAN	SCAVENGER	BUILDS NESTS
CALIFORNIA CONDOR	X	X	X	X	X	
STELLER'S SEA EAGLE	X	X	X	X		X
GREEN-HEADED TANAGER	X	X	X			X
BLACK SWIFT	X	X	X			X
PURPLE GALLINULE	X	X	X			X
TURKEY VULTURE	X	X	X	X	X	
NORTHERN MOCKINGBIRD	X	X	X			X
WHITE-TAILED TROPICBIRD	X	X	X	X		
BROWN-HEADED COWBIRD	X	X	X			

GLOSSARY

beak: the jaws and mouth of a bird. Beaks are often called bills, especially when they are long and flat.

carrion: dead and decaying flesh

crop: a pouch at the bottom of a bird's throat that stores food

endangered: likely to become extinct and no longer exist

flock: a group of birds in a particular place that belong to one species

habitat: an environment where an animal naturally lives

incubate: to keep eggs warm enough so they can hatch

omnivores: animals that eat both plants and meat

predators: animals that hunt, or prey on, other animals for food

regurgitating: bringing swallowed food back up into the mouth

scavengers: animals that eat the remains of dead animals

species: animals that share common features and can produce offspring by mating with each other

talons: sharp claws

territory: an area that is occupied and defended by an animal or a group of animals

traits: features that are inherited from parents, such as body size and feather color

wingspan: the length of a bird's wings from the tip of one wing to the tip of the other

LERNER

Expand learning beyond the printed book. Download free, complementary educational resources for this book from our website, www.lerneresource.com.

SOURCE

SELECTED BIBLIOGRAPHY

"California Condor: *Gymnogyps californianus*." The Cornell Lab of Ornithology. Accessed August 14, 2015. http://www.allaboutbirds.org/guide /California_Condor/lifehistory.

"California Condor: *Gymnogyps californianus*." San Diego Zoo Global. Accessed August 14, 2015. http://library .sandiegozoo.org/factsheets/california_ condor/condor.htm.

Lyzenga, Megan. "*Gymnogyps californianus*: California Condor."

Animal Diversity Web. Accessed August 14, 2015. http://animaldiversity.org /accounts/Gymnogyps_californianus.

Sibley, David Allen. *The Sibley Guide to Bird Life and Behavior.* New York: Chanticleer, 2001.

Tesky, Julie L. "Wildlife Species: *Gymnogyps californianus*." Fire Effects Information System. Accessed August 14, 2015. http://www.fs.fed.us/database/feis /animals/bird/gyca/all.html.

FURTHER INFORMATION

California Department of Fish and Wildlife: California Condors
https://www.dfg.ca.gov/wildlife /nongame/t_e_spp/condor
Visit this web page to learn more about California condors and how you can help protect them.

Johnson, Jinny. *Animal Planet™ Atlas of Animals*. Minneapolis: Millbrook Press, 2012. Travel around the world and explore the planet's incredible animal diversity in this richly illustrated book.

National Geographic: California Condor
http://animals.nationalgeographic.com /animals/birds/california-condor
Learn more about what California condors look like and how they behave and sound.

San Diego Zoo Animals: Andean Condor
http://animals.sandiegozoo.org/animals /condor-andean
Check out this website to learn about another kind of condor, the Andean condor.

San Diego Zoo Kids: California Condor
http://kids.sandiegozoo.org/animals /birds/california-condor
Discover interesting facts about California condors at this web page.

INDEX